# CONTENTS

# YOU GOT THIS!

Congratulations on becoming a teen! And welcome to the ultimate guide for crushing it in life! Becoming a teenager is full of excitement, wonder but also confusion. You're at that challenging stage where life throws a bunch of stuff your way.

Well, fear not, because this book has your back! It's your secret weapon for acing everything from school to social stuff and everything in between.

Inside, you'll find all sorts of awesome tips and tricks to help you handle whatever life throws your way.

Whether it's acing that test, dealing with drama, or just figuring out how to adult and keep a positive mindset.

Think of this book as your personal guide to becoming the coolest, most kick-butt version of yourself.

So, get ready to unlock your full potential, crush your goals, and slay the game of life. Let's dive in and discover the 101 Life Skills for Teens. You Got This!

# CHAPTER ONE

## BE THE BEST YOU CAN BE!

You're on an amazing journey full of new experiences, personal growth, and endless options. This chapter will talk about the most important survival skills that will help you face the challenges and take advantage of the chances that come with confidence, strength, and a sense of purpose.

Being the best you can be doesn't mean being perfect or comparing yourself to other people. It means embracing your unique strengths, passions, and beliefs while always trying to grow as a person and get better.

Each skill is like a building block on your way to becoming a better person.

You'll learn the power of setting goals, managing your time, and critical thinking along the way. This will help you get past problems, take advantage of chances, and make your life meaningful and fulfilling.

Plus you will be super knowledgeable about this stuff at such a young age that puts you way ahead of others!

So let's get started.

## 1. Goal Setting

Alright, let's start with goals – you know, those awesome things that make life exciting and keep you moving forward.

It's all about having a direction in life.

Setting goals is like creating your own personal roadmap to success, and trust me, it's way cooler than you think.

First things first, think about what really gets you pumped. Maybe it's acing that history exam, scoring a goal in soccer, or finally learning to play that guitar riff you've been obsessed with?

Whatever it is, make sure your goals line up with what you truly care about.

Now here's the secret sauce – break those big goals down into smaller, bite-sized pieces. It's like leveling up in a video game – you tackle one challenge at a time until you conquer the big boss.

## 2. Self Confidence

Imagine having someone constantly supporting and encouraging you, cheering you on at every moment. You can do this!

Here are a few suggestions to help you increase your self-confidence and feel like the amazing person you really are:

Celebrate You: Your truly unique,  be proud of it! Whether it's your great sense of humour, your love for art, or your impressive dance moves. Just remember, you're unique and that's pretty amazing!

What's Your Strong Points? We all have areas where we excel, so it's important to draw attention to those. No matter if you're great at maths, a star on the soccer pitch or a fantastic friend, be proud of your accomplishments and let them build your confidence.

## 3. Confront Your Fears

Feeling nervous or scared at times is completely normal and okay. We all have fears! However, do not allow fear to prevent you from exploring new opportunities or following your interests.

Just breathe, push yourself out of your comfort zone, and see how your confidence grows when you overcome your fears.

Visualize the other side, where do you want to be?

Create a Fear Plan:

Write a step by step on how to confront your fears and ways to manage it. This is great to refer back to if your feeling overwhelmed.

## 4. Take Lessons from Mistakes

No one is flawless, and we all make errors occasionally! Instead of getting down on yourself for errors or obstacles, view them as chances to gain knowledge and develop.

Every setback is an opportunity to pick yourself up and return with even greater resilience.

Remember it's a learning curve, so don't beat yourself up about it.

5. Overcoming Setbacks

Let's talk about setbacks – those bumps in the road that can feel like major roadblocks.

Try to see them as opportunities to level up and become even more awesome!

Think about it like this: every time you stumble, it's like a chance to learn something new and grow stronger. Maybe you bombed that math test or got turned down for a date – it happens to the best of us. But instead of dwelling on what went wrong, focus on what you can learn from the experience.

6. Finding Your Squad

Discovering your positive friends - those incredible individuals who support you, stand by you, and add a lot of joy and laughs to your life.

No matter what your interests are, there is a community out there that is eager to embrace you.

Don't hesitate to step out of your comfort zone, participate in clubs, explore new activities, and make new connections.

I understand that it may seem a bit overwhelming initially, but once you make the first move it will be easier.

Supportive friends can make you feel empowered to conquer anything!

7. Listen up to the Feedback

Let's chat about something that might sound a bit scary at first, but trust me, it's actually pretty awesome – constructive criticism and feedback.

Now, I know what you're thinking – nobody likes being told they could do better, right? But here's the thing: feedback isn't about tearing you down, it's about helping you grow.

Think of it like this: you know when you're playing a video game and you get stuck on a level? You don't just give up and stop playing, right? Nah, you keep trying until you figure it out. Well, feedback is kinda like having a cheat code that helps you level up faster.

So, the next time someone offers you some feedback – whether it's a teacher, a friend, or even your mom – take a deep breath and listen up. Because chances are, they've got some pretty valuable insights that can help you become even more awesome than you already are.

8. Dealing With Peer Pressure

Whether it's feeling pressured to do something you're not comfortable with or trying to fit in with the crowd, it can be tough to navigate.

But here's the thing: you've got way more power than you think.

Remember, you don't have to go along with the crowd if it doesn't feel right to you.

Trust your instincts, stand up for what you believe in, and surround yourself with friends who support and respect you for who you are.

Because at the end of the day, being true to yourself is the ultimate survival skill.

## 9. Resilience

That superpower that helps you bounce back from life's curveballs like a boss.

It's like having an invisible shield that protects you when things get tough.

Resilience isn't about never feeling sad, scared, or stressed — it's about knowing that even when life knocks you down, you have the strength and courage to get back up again.

So, when you're facing a challenge or feeling overwhelmed, remember that you're stronger than you think.

Take a deep breath, lean on your support system, and trust that you have what it takes to overcome anything life throws your way.

Because when it comes down to it, resilience isn't just a skill — it's a superpower that lives inside each and every one of us.

## 10. Adapting

This skill helps you roll with the punches and come out stronger on the other side.

You see, life is full of surprises, twists, and turns, and being able to adapt to whatever comes your way is key to thriving in this crazy world. YES it's a crazy world out there.

Whether it's starting a new school, trying out for a sports team, or making new friends, being adaptable means you're open to new experiences and ready to face whatever challenges come your way.

So, don't sweat the small stuff, embrace change, and remember that you've got what it takes to handle whatever life throws at you.

The possibilities are endless, and the future is full of exciting adventures just waiting to be explored.

# 11.Communication

You know, that thing we do every day without even realizing it! Here are five tips to level up your communication game:

1. Keep it Real: When you're talking to someone, whether it's your BFF or your math teacher, just be yourself. No need to put on a front or pretend to be someone you're not. Authenticity is key, and people will appreciate you for being genuine.
2. Listen Up: Communication isn't just about talking it's also about listening. So, when someone's talking to you, give them your full attention. Put down your phone, make eye contact, and really listen to what they're saying.
3. Speak Your Mind: Don't be afraid to speak up and share your thoughts and feelings. Whether you're talking to your friends, your parents, or your crush, your voice matters. So, don't hold back – say what's on your mind and speak your truth.

## 12. Time Management

Trust me, I get it – between school, sports, hanging out with friends, and maybe even a part-time job, it can feel like there just aren't enough hours in the day.

But here's the deal: with a little bit of time management magic, you can totally crush it and still have time for the stuff you love.

First things first, let's talk priorities. Figure out what's most important to you – whether it's acing that history test, killing it on the soccer field, or finally finishing that novel you've been working on.

Once you've got your priorities straight, it's time to set some goals. Break 'em down into bite-sized chunks and give yourself deadlines to keep you on track.

Now, here's the fun part – finding your groove. Maybe you're a morning person who loves to knock out homework before the sun comes up, or maybe you're more of a night owl who gets their best work done after midnight. Whatever works for you, rock it!

Just make sure you're carving out time for all the important stuff – school, sleep, and self-care included.

Oh, and don't forget to give yourself a break every now and then. Burnout is real, my friends, so make sure you're taking time to recharge your batteries and do things that make you happy.

And hey, if you ever feel like you're drowning in a sea of deadlines, don't be afraid to ask for help. Whether it's a teacher, a parent, or a friend, there are plenty of people who've got your back.

So, there you have it – a crash course in time management. With a little bit of planning, a dash of determination, and a sprinkle of self-care, you'll be slaying the time management game like a pro in no time. You've got this!

# CHAPTER TWO

## FOOD AND KITCHEN

Are you ready to bring out your inner cook and make some tasty treats at home?

You've come to the right place! We're going to dive right into the exciting world of cooking in this chapter, from learning how to use a knife to mastering some simple meals.

This part will help you feel confident in the kitchen and have fun making new dishes, no matter how much experience you have or how new you are to cooking.

So put on your apron, brush up on your cooking skills, and get ready to go on a delicious journey of learning. It's time to get better at cooking and impress your nearest and dearest!

## 13. Kitchen Basic Skills

First things first, let's talk about the building blocks of cooking – the basic techniques that will set you up for success in the kitchen. From chopping veggies like a ninja to whipping up a killer omelette, here are a few essential skills to master:

Knife Skills: Learning how to wield a knife like a pro is the secret to speeding up your prep time and avoiding kitchen mishaps. Practice your knife skills by mastering basic cuts like dicing, slicing, and mincing – your fingers will thank you!

Sautéing and Stir-Frying: Get ready to fire up the stove and unleash your inner chef! Sautéing and stir-frying are quick and versatile cooking methods that can turn simple ingredients into flavorful masterpieces. Just remember to keep the pan moving to prevent burning and achieve that perfect golden brown finish.

Boiling and Simmering: Whether you're cooking pasta, making soup, or whipping up a batch of rice, mastering the art of boiling and simmering is essential. Keep an eye on the pot, adjust the heat as needed, and you'll be on your way to perfectly cooked grains and tender veggies every time.

Baking Basics: From cookies and cakes to bread and pizza, baking opens up a world of sweet and savory possibilities. Start by mastering the basics – measuring ingredients accurately, understanding oven temperatures, and following recipes step by step.

Seasoning and Flavoring: Salt, pepper, herbs, spices – these are the secret weapons that take your dishes from bland to grand. Experiment with different seasonings and flavour combinations to discover your culinary signature!

14. Cooking on a Budget

Whether you're saving up for that dream concert ticket or just trying to stretch your allowance a little further, mastering the art of budget-friendly cooking is a total game-changer.

So put on your chef's hat and get ready to discover a world of tasty, wallet-friendly meal ideas that will have you eating like a king (or queen) without breaking the bank.

Omelettes or Frittatas: Eggs are an affordable source of protein and can be used in countless ways. Whip up a simple omelette or frittata using whatever vegetables, cheese, and leftovers you have in the fridge. It's a quick and easy meal that's perfect for breakfast, lunch, or dinner.

Homemade Sandwiches: Sandwiches are a classic budget-friendly meal option. Get creative with different breads, fillings, and spreads. You can make grilled cheese sandwiches, tuna salad sandwiches, veggie wraps, or peanut butter and banana sandwiches for a quick and satisfying meal.

Pasta Night: Pasta is not only inexpensive but also versatile. Get creative with different pasta shapes and sauces. You can make a simple tomato sauce with canned tomatoes, onions, garlic, and herbs. Add some vegetables like bell peppers, mushrooms, or spinach for extra flavor and nutrition.

Egg Fried Rice: Got some leftover rice hanging around? Turn it into a delicious egg fried rice with just a few simple ingredients. Scramble some eggs in a hot skillet, then add the cooked rice, soy sauce, and any veggies or protein you have on hand. Stir-fry until everything is heated through and you've got a tasty meal in minutes.

Homemade Pizza: Skip the pricey delivery and make your own pizza at home using store-bought pizza dough or a simple homemade crust. Load up your own pizza at home using store-bought pizza dough or a simple homemade crust. Load up your pizza with budget-friendly toppings like tomato sauce, cheese, veggies, and maybe even some leftover meat or tofu. Bake until bubbly and golden for a deliciously thrifty meal.

.

Vegetable Stir-Fry: Whip up a colorful stir-fry using whatever veggies you have on hand – think bell peppers, broccoli, carrots, and snap peas. Saute them up with some garlic and ginger, then toss with a simple soy sauce and honey dressing. Serve over rice or noodles for a satisfying meal that's both nutritious and budget-friendly.

Bean Tacos: Skip the pricey meat and opt for protein-packed beans instead. Whether it's black beans, pinto beans, or refried beans, load up your tacos with plenty of flavorful fillings like shredded lettuce, diced tomatoes, avocado slices, and a dollop of salsa. Wrap it all up in soft tortillas for a budget-friendly fiesta.

Pasta Primavera: Raid your fridge for any leftover veggies – zucchini, tomatoes, spinach, mushrooms – and toss them with cooked pasta for a quick and hearty meal. Drizzle with olive oil, sprinkle with Parmesan cheese, and season with salt, pepper, and dried herbs for a simple yet satisfying dish.

## 15. Plan Your Meals

Before hitting the grocery store, take some time to plan out your meals for the week. This will help you avoid impulse buys and ensure you only purchase what you need.

Think About Breakfast: They say it's the most important meal of the day for a reason! Choose quick and nutritious options like oatmeal with fruit, Greek yogurt with granola, or whole grain toast with peanut butter and banana.

Lunches on the Go: If you're often out and about during the day, pack portable lunches that are easy to take with you. Think wraps with veggies and hummus, pasta salad with protein like chicken or chickpeas, or a hearty grain bowl with quinoa, veggies, and a hard-boiled egg.

Avoid those impulse buys and save them for a treat!

## 16. Embrace Frozen and Canned Foods

Frozen fruits and vegetables are often just as nutritious as fresh, and they're typically more budget-friendly.

Canned beans, tomatoes, and tuna are also great

options for adding protein and flavor to your meals.

So next time you're at the grocery store, don't overlook the frozen and canned aisles.

They may not be as flashy as fresh produce, but they're definitely worth their weight in gold when it comes to convenience, affordability, and nutrition.

Get those frozen peas!

## 17. Eat the Rainbow

It can be tempting to eat and snack the same things over and over (who doesn't love their go-to?) but changing things up is what makes the magic happen.

Each food group should be seen as a different colour on your canvas, which is your plate. All of these foods—fruits, vegetables, whole grains, lean meats, and healthy fats—are great for you.

Fruits and vegetables are full of vitamins and minerals, lean foods are full of protein that helps build muscle, and avocados and nuts are full of fats that are good for your brain.

Why does it matter to have a variety?

Giving your body this is like getting a VIP pass to the best nutrition party ever. When you change things up, you make sure your body gets all the nutrients it needs to stay healthy. Also, who wants to eat the same thing every day? When you mix things up, your taste buds stay happy and your meals stay interesting.

## 18. Hydrate

You could think of water as your magic potion; it gives you superpowers and keeps your skin glowing, brain sharp, and energy levels high. It's also the best way to cool down after a tough workout or a day in the sun. How can you be sure you drink enough water?

First things first, get rid of the sweets. You know, those sneaky beers and sports drinks that say they'll give you a quick boost but then make you crash later. Pick something like water, herbal tea, or flavoured water drinks instead. They taste great and also keep you hydrated without making your blood sugar drop.

As a bonus, remember to bring a reusable water bottle with you all the time. Having water on hand makes it easy to stay hydrated all day, whether you're studying, hanging out with friends, or killing it at practice.

Your body will be grateful, and you'll be ready for anything that comes your way. Cheers to drinking water!

19. Limit Processed Foods

We get it—it's hard to say no to the ease of use, the taste, and the quick gratification. But here's the truth: finding that balance is key to good health.

It's fine to enjoy treats once in a while; after all, life is too short not to enjoy a sweet or savoury snack now and then. But here's the catch: those highly prepared foods, like sugary snacks, fast food burgers, and meals that come in a box? In the world of diet, they're like the bad guys. They may taste good at the time, but they're not good for you because they're full of bad fats, sugars, and enough sodium to make your taste buds twist.

What's the deal? Keeping things in check is key. Try not to eat those processed foods all the time. Instead, save them for special events or treats once in a while. Healthy fats, whole grains, lean meats, and fresh fruits and vegetables are like superheroes in the world of nutrition. They'll make you feel like a million bucks.

## 20. Host a Come Dine with Me

Let's turn up the heat in the kitchen and make cooking an epic adventure with your friends! Who says whipping up meals has to be a solo mission?

Gather your squad, turn on some tunes, and get ready for a culinary showdown that'll rival the pros. Imagine this – you and your friends hosting your very own "Come Dine with Me" or "MasterChef" competition right in your kitchen. Each of you gets to showcase your skills and creativity by cooking up a storm and presenting your dishes to the judging panel (aka your friends).

But wait, it gets better – you can even take turns hosting themed dinner parties where everyone brings their A-game and cooks a dish based on the chosen theme.

Whether it's a Mexican fiesta, Italian feast, or sushi extravaganza, the possibilities are endless!

## 21. Leftovers Rule

Those unsung heroes of the kitchen that often get overlooked but hold the key to some seriously tasty meals! You know those nights when you've got a bit of this and a bit of that lurking in the fridge? Well, it's time to turn those leftovers into a culinary masterpiece!

Think of leftovers as your secret weapon in the kitchen – they're like a treasure trove of ingredients just waiting to be transformed into something delicious. Got some leftover roasted veggies from last night's dinner? Throw them into a stir-fry with some protein and a splash of soy sauce for a quick and easy meal.

The best part? Leftovers are totally customizable, so you can let your creativity run wild! Mix and match ingredients, experiment with different flavors, and don't be afraid to get a little adventurous.

Who knows – you might just stumble upon your new favorite recipe!

## 22. Portion Control

Let's chat about portion control – it's like the secret sauce to feeling awesome and energized throughout the day! Here's the scoop:

You know those times when you're digging into a delicious meal and suddenly realize you've eaten enough to feed a small army?

We've all been there! But here's the thing – paying attention to portion sizes can make a world of difference when it comes to feeling satisfied and keeping your energy levels in check.

Picture this: imagine your plate as a canvas, and each food group as a different colour. You've got your veggies, your protein, your carbs, and your healthy fats – all coming together to create a masterpiece of a meal. But here's the trick – you want to make sure you're not overloading your plate with too much of one thing.

Instead, aim for a balanced mix of protein, carbs, and fats in every meal.

## 23. Clean Up!

Keeping your kitchen spick and span – because a clean kitchen is a happy kitchen!

Picture this: you're whipping up your favorite meal, jamming out to your favorite tunes, and feeling like a culinary rockstar. But hold up – before you dive into cooking mode, it's time to give your kitchen a little TLC.

First things first, wash those hands! Yep, you heard me right – scrub those mitts with soap and water for at least 20 seconds before you start cooking.

Next up, it's all about keeping those surfaces squeaky clean. Grab a sponge or a cloth and give your countertops, cutting boards, and utensils a good wipe down with hot, soapy water.

Last but not least, let's talk dishes. I know, I know – nobody loves doing dishes. But trust me, it's worth it! Wash your dishes promptly after using them to avoid any funky smells or, heaven forbid, moldy surprises.

So there you have it, folks – the key to a happy, healthy kitchen is all about cleanliness.

# CHAPTER THREE

## MONEY AND BUDGETING

Welcome to the ultimate crash course in money management – where we're about to dive headfirst into the world of budgeting, saving, and all things finance.

Now, I know what you're thinking – money talk? Yawn. But trust me, mastering the art of budgeting isn't just about counting pennies and pinching pennies. It's about taking control of your financial future, making your money work for you, and setting yourself up for success, both now and down the road.

In this chapter, we're going to cover everything you need to know to become a bona fide money master. From understanding the basics of budgeting to creating a financial plan that works for you, we've got you covered.

So buckle up, because by the time we're done here, you'll be ready to tackle anything that comes your way – financially speaking, that is. Let's dive in!

## 24. The Basics of Money

Alright, teens, let's break it down – survival skills for navigating the financial jungle! First up, we're talking about income – that's the dough you bring in from babysitting, mowing lawns, or that part-time gig at the local café. Knowing how to hustle and earn your keep is like having a secret superpower in the real world.

Next, let's tackle expenses – the stuff you shell out your hard-earned cash on. From that must-have pair of sneakers to grabbing lunch with friends, expenses can add up fast.

But fear not! Learning to distinguish between needs (like food and shelter) and wants (like the latest tech gadgets) is key to keeping your wallet happy and your bank account in check.

And now, drumroll please – budgeting! Think of budgeting as your trusty survival toolkit for financial success.

## 25. Financial Goals

Ready to embark on a thrilling adventure into the world of financial goal-setting? Strap in, because we're about to make setting financial goals as fun as a rollercoaster ride at your favorite theme park. Here's your step-by-step guide to becoming a financial goal-setting superstar:

Dream Big: Start by unleashing your imagination and dreaming up your wildest financial fantasies. Want to save up for that dream vacation, snag the latest gaming console, or maybe even start your own business? The sky's the limit, so let your imagination run wild!

Get Specific: Now that you've got your dreams locked and loaded, it's time to get down to the nitty-gritty. Get specific about your goals – how much money do you need, and by when? Whether it's $500 for that concert ticket or $5,000 for a down payment on your first car, be crystal clear about what you're aiming for.

.

- Break it Down: Next up, let's break those big, juicy goals into bite-sized chunks. Divide your goal into smaller milestones or checkpoints along the way. It's like leveling up in your favorite video game – each milestone brings you one step closer to victory!

- Make a Plan: Now that you've got your roadmap to financial glory, it's time to make a plan of attack. Figure out how much money you need to save each week or month to reach your goals on time. You could even create a colorful chart or use a budgeting app to track your progress – who said budgeting had to be boring?

- Stay Motivated: Last but not least, let's keep that motivation train chugging along. Celebrate your wins along the way – whether it's hitting a savings milestone or resisting the urge to splurge on impulse buys. And don't forget to visualize your success – imagine yourself lounging on that beach or cruising in your brand-new wheels. With a little determination and a lot of imagination, you'll be crushing your financial goals in no time!

## 26. Budgeting

Budgeting isn't just about pinching pennies and counting coins; it's about empowering yourself to make smart financial decisions that set you up for success.

We will show you how to track your income and expenses like a pro, create a budgeting plan that suits your lifestyle, and make every dollar count towards your financial goals.

And hey, we get it – life can throw some unexpected curveballs your way. That's why we'll also cover strategies for handling those surprise expenses and building up an emergency fund to keep you covered when life gets a little wild.

Get to Know Your Money: First, make a list of all the money that comes in every month. That's your money, whether it comes from babysitting, a part-time job, or your wonderful salary.

.Keep an eye on your stacks: Next, keep an eye on where your money is going. Write down everything you spend money on, from your daily latte to performance tickets for you and your friends. It's easy to keep track of things with apps like Mint and PocketGuard.

Make some plans: Let's begin to dream! How much money do you want to make? Clear goals keep you going when you're saving for something like a new phone, a weekend trip, or college.

Split It Up: It's time to split up that dough! You should set aside some of your cash to pay for things like food, transportation, and savings. Don't forget to leave room for fun things too!

Don't Change: You can only make a budget work if you follow it. Watch your savings grow as you keep track of your spending and make changes as needed.

27. Smart Spending

Let's chat about being wizards of smart spending – trust me, it's like unlocking the cheat codes to financial freedom!

Picture this: you're cruising down the aisles of your favorite store, eyeing that shiny new gadget or killer outfit. But hold up – before you hit that "buy now" button, let's sprinkle some magic on those spending habits!

.

First trick up our sleeves: savvy shopping! Think like a detective – scour for deals, compare prices, and hunt down those sweet discounts. Whether it's using coupons, shopping during sales, or even hitting up thrift stores for hidden treasures, smart shopping is all about snagging the best bang for your buck.

Now, let's talk about the villain of the story – impulse buys. We've all been there – that sudden urge to splurge on something totally unnecessary.

Before you whip out that wallet, take a breath and ask yourself: "Do I really need this?" Channel your inner Jedi and resist the dark side of impulse buying.

Instead, focus on your goals – whether it's saving up for that dream vacation or scoring those concert tickets. Remember, every dollar saved brings you one step closer to your financial dreams.

So there you have it your guide to mastering the art of smart spending! With a little strategy and a sprinkle of magic, you'll be stretching those dollars and living your best financial life in no time.

May the frugal force be with you!

## 28. Earning and Saving

We're diving into the world of earning and saving, and trust me, it's gonna be epic!

So, you're itching to beef up that bank account? Well, guess what – you've got more options than a superhero's arsenal! From snagging part-time gigs at your local coffee joint to flexing those entrepreneurial muscles with your own business idea, the world is your oyster when it comes to making moolah.

But wait, it gets even better – we're not just talking about raking in the dough; we're also about stacking those stacks! Yep, we're talking about the magical art of saving.

Picture this: every dollar you stash away today is like planting seeds for your future financial forest. So whether you're eyeing that dream car or dreaming of jet-setting across the globe, start squirreling away those savings like a boss.

Let's explore some epic ways you can earn money and level up your financial game:

.

Part-Time Jobs: If you want to make extra money, look for part-time jobs at nearby shops, restaurants, or coffee shops. You'll get paid, learn new skills, and meet new people along the way.

Freelance Work: Do you really know how to use social media, write, or make graphics? Try your hand at being creative and look for independent work. You can find great gigs that match your skills and hobbies on sites like Upwork, Fiverr, and Freelancer.

Spirit of an Entrepreneur: You have a million-dollar business idea in your head. Start your own small business and let your inner businessman out! There are a lot of things you can do, like selling crafts you made yourself, tutoring, or starting a YouTube programme.

Care for children and pets: Do you love kids or pets? You can have fun and make money by babysitting or taking care of pets. Get the word out to family, neighbours, and friends, or sign up on sites like Care.com or Rover that will help you babysit and take care of pets.

Odd Jobs: The list of odd jobs you can do to make extra money is long. They range from mowing the lawn and shovelling snow to walking the dog and cleaning the house. Post flyers or use community bulletin boards to let people know about your services.

Get rid of your stuff: Get rid of things you don't need or use and make some extra cash by selling them. Sites like eBay, Depop, and Facebook Marketplace make it easy to sell your unwanted items for cash. You can sell clothes, books, gadgets, or souvenirs.

Follow Through: Making a budget only works if you do what you say you will do. Watch your savings grow as you keep track of your spending and make changes as needed.

Sure, it might be tempting to blow every dollar on the latest gadgets or coolest experiences, but trust me – there's serious power in padding your piggy bank. Here's why:

Big Dreams, Big Savings: Ever dreamt of traveling the world, starting your own business, or buying your dream car? Well, guess what – those dreams are totally within reach when you start squirreling away your savings. Every dollar you save today is like planting seeds for your future goals and aspirations.

Emergency Safety Net: Life's full of surprises – and not all of them are good. Whether it's unexpected car repairs, medical bills, or sudden job loss, having a solid savings cushion can be a total lifesaver when life throws you a curveball. Think of it as your own personal superhero cape, ready to swoop in and save the day when you need it most.

Financial Freedom: Imagine a life where you call the shots, instead of being at the mercy of your bank account. That's the power of financial freedom – and it all starts with saving.

Whether it's having the freedom to pursue your passions, take risks, or weather life's ups and downs without breaking a sweat, saving gives you the keys to unlock the door to your dreams.

So, let's make a pact to start stashing away those savings like there's no tomorrow. With a little discipline, determination, and a whole lot of saving smarts, you'll be well on your way to a brighter, more secure future.

.

## 29. Managing Debt

Let's chat about a topic that might not be the most glamorous, but trust me, it's a biggie – managing debt. Now, I know what you're thinking – debt sounds like a total buzzkill, right?

But here's the deal: understanding how to handle debt responsibly is like wielding a superpower that can set you up for financial success down the road. So, let's tackle one of the biggest beasts in the debt jungle – student loans.

Picture this: you're off to college, ready to tackle the world and chase your dreams. But along with that diploma comes a hefty price tag – student loans. Now, before you panic, let's break it down. Student loans can be a powerful tool for investing in your education and future career, but they come with serious responsibility. Here's the lowdown:

Know Your Loans: First things first, understand what kind of student loans you have – federal, private, subsidized, unsubsidized – and the terms and conditions of each. Knowledge is power, my friends!

Borrow Wisely: Sure, it might be tempting to borrow the max amount offered, but think twice before you sign on the dotted line. Remember, every dollar you borrow now is a dollar you'll have to pay back later – with interest!

Make a Plan: Once you graduate, it's game time. Make a game plan for tackling those student loans head-on. Consider your repayment options, like income-driven repayment plans or refinancing, and choose the strategy that works best for you.

Stay on Track: Don't let those student loans linger like a bad hangover. Stay on top of your payments, stick to your budget, and avoid falling behind. Trust me, your future self will thank you!

So, don't let student loans scare you off from chasing your dreams. With a little know-how and a whole lot of hustle, you can conquer that debt mountain and emerge victorious on the other side. Here's to crushing those student loans like the financial warriors you are!

## 30. Planning for the Future

Let's talk about making plans for the future, because you know what? You are just beginning your financial journey, and it's never too early to plan out how you will get there. Setting smart financial goals is important whether you want to go on trips in college, get your own car, or even just relax in retirement (yes, really!).

Let's picture this: you have big plans, right? You need a plan to make those dreams come true. Right now is the time to start planning your next steps, whether they involve saving money for college, a cool ride, or even your golden years. The good news is that you're not alone! Our deep dive into the world of financial literacy will give you the information and skills to handle the ups and downs of your financial journey like a boss.

Get ready for the grand journey of long-term financial planning. Be sure to buckle up and strap in. A little planning, some smart money moves, and a lot of hard work will get you close to making your future dreams come true. Let's get it done! 💪

# CHAPTER FOUR

## SOCIAL SKILLS

So, what are social skills, anyway?

Basically, they're like your superpowers for interacting with other humans – whether it's making new friends, chatting with your crush, or handling sticky situations like a boss.

And the cool thing is, these skills aren't just for making small talk at parties (although they totally come in handy for that too) – they're legit life skills that'll set you up for success in school, work, and beyond. But here's the best part – mastering social skills isn't about being the coolest kid in the room or having a million followers on Insta.

It's about being your authentic self, connecting with others in a genuine way, and showing kindness and respect to everyone you meet. So buckle up, because we're about to embark on a wild ride through the wonderful world of social skills – and trust me, it's gonna be epic!

## 31. Being Empathetic

How can you make kindness a part of your daily life? A starting point is to actively listen and pay attention to what other people are saying and how they feel. Listen carefully and let the person know that you understand when they talk about their good or bad times.

To move on, try to picture how you would feel if you were them. This shows that you care about them and helps you understand how they feel. Remember that empathy isn't about solving someone else's problems; it's about being there for them and helping them understand.

Lastly, be kind and caring to other people when you talk to them. Small acts of kindness, like being there for someone to talk to or lean on, can make their day and the relationships you have with those around you stronger.

## 32. Maintaining Friends

Let's talk friendships – because having a squad that's got your back is like having your own personal hype team! Making and maintaining friendships is all about finding your tribe.

So, how do you do it? Well, first off, be yourself! Seriously, there's no need to pretend to be someone you're not – the right friends will dig you just the way you are.

Next, put yourself out there! Join clubs, sports teams, or community groups where you can meet people who share your interests.

And once you've found your crew, keep the love alive by being there for each other through thick and thin. Remember, friendships take effort, so don't be afraid to reach out, check in, and show your pals some love.

With a little bit of kindness, authenticity, and a whole lot of laughter, you'll build friendships that last a lifetime. So go ahead, make those connections, and watch your squad grow stronger every day!

## 33. Digital Savvy

Hey, tech-savvy teens, let's chat about digital etiquette and communication – because in today's digital world, knowing how to navigate the online realm is key to keeping it real!

Digital etiquette, or "netiquette" if you wanna get fancy, is all about treating others with respect and kindness in the digital sphere. So, what does that look
l

like? Well, for starters, think before you post!

Remember that what you say online can have a real impact on others, so always choose your words wisely and avoid spreading negativity or drama.

Oh, and speaking of drama, don't get sucked into online conflicts or cyberbullying – just hit that block button and keep it moving. And when it comes to communication, keep it clear, concise, and courteous.

By being mindful of your online behavior and communicating with respect, you'll build positive relationships and create a safe and supportive online community for everyone. So let's keep it classy, keep it kind, and keep the digital vibes positive!

34. Assertiveness

Let's talk about assertiveness versus aggressiveness – because knowing the difference can be a game-changer when it comes to standing up for yourself and others.

Assertiveness is all about expressing your thoughts, feelings, and needs in a confident and respectful way, without stepping on anyone else's toes. It's like speaking your truth with confidence and setting boundaries like a boss.

On the flip side, aggressiveness is more about bulldozing your way through situations, often at the expense of others' feelings or rights. It's like trying to win at all costs, even if it means steamrolling over everyone else.

So, how can you be assertive without crossing the line into aggressiveness?

Well, it's all about finding that sweet spot – speaking up for yourself and standing your ground, but also being open to listening to others' perspectives and finding common ground.

35. Respect For Others

Respect is like the glue that holds everything together in a relationship. It's what builds trust, understanding, and help for each other. Respecting each other is important for making healthy, happy relationships with people, whether they're friends, family, or a romantic partner.

So, how does respect show up in real life?

It means respecting each other's feelings, thoughts, and limits, even if you don't agree with them. It means constantly listening, being open and honest with each other, and being there for each other in good times and bad.

And maybe most importantly, it's about seeing how valuable each other is and being kind, understanding, and caring to each other.

When you treat people with respect, you make the space where they feel safe and supported, where everyone feels heard and respected. Remember that respect is the most important thing in all of our interactions.

36. Networking

It's never too early to start setting yourself up for future job success by networking and making professional connections.

Making connections and getting to know people who can help you with your job is what networking is all about. These people could be mentors, teachers, or professionals in your field.

What should you do to begin?

Start by putting yourself out there. Go to career fairs, join clubs or groups that are related to your hobbies, and don't be shy about asking people you look up to for help or advice.

Don't forget that networking isn't just about getting things from other people; it's also about giving. Being real, interested, and ready to learn from others is important.

37. Dealing with Conflict

Let's face it, disagreements are just a part of life, right?

But here's the thing – how you handle those conflicts can make all the difference. So, when tensions start to rise, take a deep breath and remember to keep your cool. Instead of jumping straight into the heat of the moment, try to step back and see the situation from the other person's perspective. Listening is key here, folks!

Once you understand where they're coming from, it's easier to find common ground and work towards a solution that works for everyone. And hey, don't be afraid to speak up for yourself and express how you're feeling – just keep it respectful and constructive.

By approaching conflicts with an open mind, empathy, and a willingness to find compromise, you'll not only resolve the issue at hand but also strengthen your relationships in the process.

So let's keep the peace, folks – because life's too short for unnecessary drama!

## 38. Active Listening

When someone is talking, you should give them your full attention and not let your phone, thoughts, or other things going on around you get in the way.

Listen to what the other person has to say instead of just waiting your turn to talk. How then can you be a good listener? Make eye contact, nod your head, and say things like "uh-huh" or "I see" to show that you're interested in what they're saying.

Don't forget to ask questions and really listen to what the other person has to say; it's like sitting in the front row of their own story!

If you learn how to actively listen, you'll quickly become a great communicator who can make connections and improve relationships. It's time to step up your listening skills and rock those talks like a boss!

## 39. Responding to Bullying

Let's talk about recognizing and responding to bullying – because no one deserves to feel unsafe or unwelcome in their own space, right?

First things first, it's important to know that bullying comes in many forms, from hurtful words and teasing to physical violence and cyberbullying.

If you or someone you know is being bullied, it's essential to speak up and seek help from a trusted adult or authority figure.

Remember, you're not alone – there are people who care about you and want to support you through this. And if you see bullying happening to someone else, don't be a bystander – speak out, offer support, and report it to someone who can help.

Together, we can create a culture of kindness and respect where everyone feels safe and valued. So let's stand up to bullying, support each other, and create a world where everyone can thrive.

40. Boundaries and Saying NO!

Knowing your limits is important for taking care of yourself and keeping relationships healthy.

Setting limits means being clear with others about what you can and can't handle, whether it's in a friendship, a relationship, or your family.

It can be hard to say "no," especially when you want to avoid strife or make other people happy, but it's important to put your own needs first and stand up for yourself.

Always remember that it's okay to say no to things that don't fit with your ideals, make you feel bad, or aren't right for you. If someone doesn't respect your boundaries or tries to force you to do something you don't want to, don't be afraid to stand up for yourself and set clear limits.

People should treat you with respect and honour your feelings. Don't give up, speak up, and remember that it's okay to put yourself first sometimes. You can do this.

# CHAPTER FIVE

## PROBLEM SOLVING &
## DECISION MAKING

Ready to level up your problem-solving and decision-making skills?

Because let's be real – life's full of tricky situations and tough choices, and knowing how to tackle them like a pro can make all the difference.

Whether you're facing a sticky social dilemma, trying to figure out your next career move, or just navigating the ups and downs of everyday life, having solid problem-solving and decision-making skills in your toolkit is key to thriving in any situation.

Get ready to unleash your inner problem-solving genius and make decisions like a boss – because with the right skills and a little bit of know-how, there's no problem you can't solve and no decision you can't make with confidence. Let's do this!

## 41. Problem Solving

Let's dive into understanding problem-solving – because life's a bit like a puzzle, right?

Sometimes, you've got to figure out how to piece everything together to make it work. Problem-solving is all about using your smarts, creativity, and perseverance to tackle challenges head-on and find solutions that work for you.

Whether it's dealing with drama with your pals, nailing that tricky math problem, or finding your way through a maze of options for your future, problem-solving skills are your secret weapon for overcoming obstacles and coming out on top.

So, get ready to flex those mental muscles, think outside the box, and take on whatever life throws your way like the problem-solving pro that you are.

## 42. Challenges in Teen Life

Let's talk about identifying challenges in teen life – because let's face it, being a teenager isn't always smooth sailing.

From navigating friendships and relationships to dealing with academic stress and figuring out who you are and what you want in life, there's no shortage of hurdles to overcome. But here's the thing – by recognizing and understanding the challenges you face, you're already one step closer to finding solutions and mastering those survival skills.

So take a moment to reflect on what's been giving you a hard time lately – whether it's feeling overwhelmed by schoolwork, struggling to fit in, or dealing with family issues.

1. Academic Pressure: Balancing homework, exams, and extracurricular activities can be stressful.
2. Peer Pressure: Feeling pressured to fit in or engage in risky behaviors to gain acceptance.
3. Self-Identity: Figuring out who you are, your values, and where you fit in the world.
4. Relationships: Navigating friendships, romantic relationships, and family dynamics.
5. Body Image: Dealing with societal pressures and expectations regarding physical appearance.
6. Mental Health: Coping with stress, anxiety, depression, or other mental health issues.
7. Time Management: Juggling school, hobbies, social life, and personal responsibilities.
8. Future Uncertainty: Deciding on career paths, college choices, or life after high school.

9.Technology Overload: Managing screen time, social media, and online interactions.
10.Peer Conflict: Resolving conflicts with friends or peers in school or social settings.

## 43. Academic Challenges

Let's Break it Down: If you have a hard problem or project, divide it into smaller tasks that you can handle better. Taking things one step at a time can help the whole project seem less scary.

Do not be afraid to ask for help from teachers, classmates, or trainers when you are having trouble. It's not a sign of weakness to ask questions and get more information.

Make Good Use of Resources: Use the tools you have access to, like textbooks, online study tools, and educational websites. If you use these tools, you can better understand what you are learning.

Keep track of your assignments, due dates, and study tools to avoid feeling too busy. You can stay on track by making a study plan and blocking off time to do your homework and study.

Practice Critical Thinking: To improve your critical thinking skills, look at information, proof, and come to logical conclusions. This will not only help you solve problems better, but it will also help you do better in school generally.

## 44. Boost Confidence

Confidence isn't about always being right or never making mistakes; it's about believing in yourself and your ability to navigate life's twists and turns with courage and resilience.

So, how do you boost that confidence muscle? Start by getting to know yourself – your strengths, your passions, and your values.

When you're clear on who you are and what matters most to you, it's easier to trust your instincts and make choices that align with your authentic self.

And remember, it's okay to seek advice from trusted mentors or friends, but ultimately, the power to choose is yours. So own your decisions, embrace the journey, and trust that even if things don't always go as planned, you've got the skills and the strength to handle whatever comes your way.

## 45. Decision Making for Goals

Let's talk about how to make choices that will help you reach your future goals. Your dreams are worth chasing, and each choice you make today shapes the way you end up tomorrow.

It's important to picture the future you want and take steps to make it come true, whether you're thinking about what to study in college, your job, or where to focus your energy and skills.

Start by making goals that are clear, attainable, and inspire you to achieve. Then, break your big dreams down into smaller jobs that you can do one at a time.

Also, don't be afraid to try new things, take risks, and be open to the unknown. Sometimes the best choices are the ones that take you down exciting and unexpected roads. Believe that you can reach your future goals if you have courage and drive. Dare to dream big and aim high. You have the whole world to yourself; go make it happen!

## 46. Creative Problem Solving

Sometimes, thinking outside the box is the key to unlocking solutions you never knew existed!

Creative problem-solving is all about flexing those mental muscles and approaching challenges with an open mind and a sprinkle of imagination.

So, next time you're faced with a tricky situation, why not try brainstorming a list of wild and wacky ideas? You never know – that seemingly crazy concept might just be the spark that ignites the perfect solution!

And hey, don't be afraid to collaborate with friends or bounce ideas off each other – sometimes, two heads (or three, or four!) are better than one.

So embrace your inner creativity, think outside the lines, and remember that there's no problem too big or too small that a little imagination can't solve.

## 47. Solving Conflict with Peers

When tensions arise with friends or peers, it's important to approach the situation with empathy, patience, and a willingness to listen.

Start by calmly expressing your thoughts and feelings, and be open to hearing the other person's perspective.

Remember, it's okay to disagree – what matters most is how you work together to find common ground and move forward. So, whether it's a disagreement over who gets the last slice of pizza or a more serious issue, like hurt feelings or misunderstandings, take a deep breath, keep communication lines open, and approach the situation with kindness and respect.

By practicing effective communication and problem-solving skills, you'll not only resolve conflicts peacefully but also strengthen your friendships and social connections along the way.

48. Mental Health

Coping with stress, anxiety, depression, or other mental health issues can feel overwhelming, but know that you're not alone, and there are ways to navigate these challenges.

First off, it's okay to not be okay sometimes – we all have our ups and downs, and it's important to give yourself permission to feel your feelings without judgment.

When things get tough, don't hesitate to reach out for support – whether it's talking to a trusted friend, family member, or school counselor, or seeking professional help if needed.

Remember, you're stronger than you think, and there's always hope, even on the darkest days. So take it one step at a time, practice self-care, and know that brighter days are ahead.

## 49. Stand Up for Your Choices

Let's talk about how important it is to think about and learn from the choices we make.

Every choice, no matter how big or small, is a chance to grow and learn more about ourselves. When you think about the choices you've made, you're not just remembering the past; you're also making plans for the future.

Whenever you are at a crossroads or have to make a tough choice, take a moment to think about what you can do and what might happen. Then, believe your gut. Hey, it's okay if things don't go as planned!

Do not let those bad events hold you back. Instead, use them to make you stronger and better. Always keep in mind that life is a journey and that each choice you make is a step towards your goals. So go with the flow, stay true to who you are, and keep learning and growing as you go.

# CHAPTER SIX

## NAVIGATING THE WORLD

So, picture this: you've got Google Maps open on your phone, right? It's like having a superpower that lets you explore the world without ever leaving your bedroom.

But hey, there's more to navigating life than just figuring out the quickest route to Starbucks.

We're gonna talk about learning new languages — not just the ones you study in school, but the languages of different cultures and experiences.

Because let's face it, being able to connect with people from all walks of life is a pretty awesome skill to have.

## 50. Learn a Language

I know what you're thinking – why bother when we've got Google Translate, right? But trust me, there's so much more to it than just being able to order a pizza in French.

Learning a new language opens up a whole new world of possibilities. It's like unlocking a secret code that lets you connect with people from all over the globe, discover new cultures, and see the world in a whole new way. Plus, it's a killer way to impress your friends and stand out on college applications.

But here's the best part – you don't have to be a language genius to start learning. Whether you're brushing up on your high school Spanish or diving headfirst into Mandarin Chinese, there are tons of apps, websites, and resources out there to help you on your language-learning journey.

So, what are you waiting for? Pick a language that speaks to you (pun totally intended), set some goals, and dive in!

## 51. Learn Basic Survival Skills

You may have seen Bear Grylls tackle the wild on TV, drinking his own pee and eating insects to survive. While his extreme adventures might seem a bit over the top, there's something to be said about the importance of learning basic survival skills.

Sure, you might not find yourself stranded in the middle of nowhere with only a water bottle and a knife, but knowing how to build a shelter, find water, and signal for help could come in handy in unexpected situations.

Think of it like leveling up in a video game – the more skills you have, the better equipped you are to handle whatever life throws your way. So, take a page from Bear Grylls' book (figuratively, of course) and start learning those basic survival skills. You never know when they might just save the day!

## 52. Respect the Environment

It's not enough to just have fun when you're outside exploring. You should also take care of the earth. As a guest in someone else's house, you should leave it as good as you found it, if not better!

This is where the Leave No Trace ideas come in.

The whole point is to have as little of an effect on nature as possible so that future generations can enjoy it too.

Remember to stay on marked trails, keep your distance from wildlife, and leave only your tracks behind when you're hiking, camping, or just hanging out in nature.

Also, don't forget to throw away trash the right way —no one wants to find their trash while they're enjoying the outdoors.

By following the Leave No Trace rules, you not only show that you care about nature, but you also show others how to do the same. Let's all do what we can to protect the Earth's beauty for future generations!

53. Plan Your Route

Grab a map and a compass (or your phone with offline maps), and start plotting your course. Look for key landmarks like lakes, mountains, or trail junctions to help you stay on track.

Check for trail markers or signs along the way to keep you headed in the right direction. And don't forget to scout out potential hazards, like steep cliffs or river crossings, so you can steer clear of trouble

By planning your route ahead of time, you'll not only stay safe but also make the most of your outdoor adventure. So, grab your gear and get ready to blaze your own trail – the great outdoors is waiting!

54. Seek Adventure

At the edge of a forest, you hold a map in your hand and a compass on your belt. You look around with a sense of wonder in your eyes. The world is your playground, and now that you know how to navigate and be outside, there is no terrain that you can't handle.

Enjoy the thrill of finding new things as you walk along secret trails, through beautiful mountains, and along twisting rivers. With each step, you'll get better at survival, being able to easily find your way through thick woods and rough terrain. But it's not just about getting good at the wilderness; it's also about finding your own strength, guts, and toughness.

It's time to go on a trip! Put your hiking boots on and fill your rucksack with the things you need. There are many ways to have an adventure: climbing peaks, sleeping under the stars, or paddling down winding rivers. Each one gives you a chance to test your limits, make experiences that will last a lifetime.

## 55. Get Clued Up : First Aid

Let's talk about a skill that could truly be a lifesaver: administering first aid. Picture yourself on a hike with friends or at a sports game when suddenly someone twists an ankle or gets a cut. Knowing how to administer first aid means you can step in and provide immediate care until professional help arrives.

Think of it as adding a superhero tool to your belt. Whether it's treating minor cuts and scrapes, tabilizing a sprained ankle, or knowing what to do in more serious situations like a broken bone or allergic reaction, having basic first aid skills can make a big difference.

Plus, it's not as complicated as it sounds! You can learn the basics through classes, online resources, or even by practicing with friends and family. And the best part? You'll gain confidence knowing that you're prepared to handle unexpected injuries and emergencies, whether you're out in the wilderness, at home, or anywhere else life takes you.

## 56. Start a Fire

Picture yourself camping with friends or going for a walk in the woods as the sun goes down and the nights get cooler. If you know how to start a fire, you can stay warm, cook food, and even call for help if you need to.

But wait, don't get scared! It's not as hard as it sounds to start a fire. You can learn many ways to use the sun's power, such as rubbing sticks together (yes, just like in the movies!) or using fire starters or magnifying glasses. Like getting good at a magic trick that can save the day!

Also, making a fire isn't just a safety skill; it's also fun to learn and use. Get some people together, build a campfire, and show them how good you are at starting fires.

Just remember to stay safe at all times and follow the right fire safety rules. You'll be able to start fires like a pro in no time if you practise!

## 57. Volunteer

Let's talk about one of the most underrated survival skills out there – volunteering. I know, I know, your schedule is already jam-packed with school, sports, and social stuff, but trust me, carving out some time to give back can be a game-changer.

Volunteering isn't just about racking up community service hours for your college application (although that's definitely a bonus!). It's about making a real difference in the world and connecting with your community in a meaningful way. Whether you're tutoring kids at a local elementary school, cleaning up a beach, or serving meals at a homeless shelter, every little bit counts.

But here's the thing – volunteering isn't just good for the world, it's good for you too. It boosts your confidence, builds empathy, and gives you a sense of purpose like nothing else. Plus, it's a killer way to meet new people, gain valuable skills, and even explore potential career paths.

So, next time you're feeling stressed or overwhelmed, why not take a break from Instagram scrolling and give back instead?

## 58. Have a Mindful Mind

Life can be hard in many ways, from tests and relationships to just navigating the ups and downs of daily life. This is where being aware comes in handy.

Mindfulness is like going to the gym for your mind. Just like going to the gym to build muscle, it helps you feel better mentally and emotionally. Even when things get hard, you need to learn how to stay calm, focused, and in the moment.

How do you do it? To do this, all you have to do is take a few deep breaths, find a quiet place to meditate, or even do some visualization techniques. These techniques may sound hard to learn, but they're really simple and can make a big difference in how you deal with problems and stress.

Imagine having a secret superpower that helps you handle stress, get back on your feet after a loss, and handle anything life throws at you with poise and confidence. That's the power of being aware and strong. So why not give it a shot? It will be good for you in the long run.

## 59. Get Cultured

I know, it might sound a bit intimidating at first, but trust me, it's totally worth stepping out of your comfort zone for.

Experiencing different cultures isn't just about checking off items on your travel bucket list (although that's definitely part of the fun!).

It's about opening your mind to new ideas, perspectives, and ways of life. Whether you're trying exotic foods at a local cultural festival, learning traditional dances from around the world, or exploring historical landmarks in far-off lands, every cultural experience is a chance to broaden your horizons and expand your worldview.

So go ahead, embrace the diversity around you, and get ready for the adventure of a lifetime. Because when you open yourself up to new cultures, you're not just surviving – you're thriving!

# CHAPTER SEVEN

## COPING WITH EMOTIONS

Welcome to a chapter all about mastering the art of coping with emotions.

Buckle up because we're diving deep into the wild and wonderful world of feelings.

From the highs of happiness to the lows of sadness, we'll be exploring how to ride the rollercoaster of emotions with grace and resilience.

So, if you've ever felt like your emotions were a tangled ball of yarn, fear not! By the end of this chapter, you'll have the tools and techniques to unravel those knots, understand what makes you tick, and emerge stronger and more self-aware than ever before.

Get ready to embark on an epic journey of self-discovery and emotional empowerment – let's dive in!

## 60. Feelings

Hey teens, let's dive into the world of feelings.

Knowing how you feel is the first thing that will help you handle the ups and downs of life like a pro! Each emotion is different and important in its own way, just like each colour of the rainbow.

You can feel everything, from happiness and excitement to sadness and anger. Now, take a moment to pay attention to how you feel.

Are you really excited about something that's coming up, or are you feeling down after a hard day at school?

No matter what it is, know that it's okay to feel everything. Your feelings are what make you uniquely beautiful. Also, remember that you're not alone if you ever need help figuring out how to deal with something or what you're feeling. Life is an emotional roller coaster that we'll ride together, one feeling at a time.

## 61. Triggers

Let's talk about recognizing triggers and patterns in our emotions — because understanding what sets off those emotional fireworks is the first step toward taking control of our inner world.

Think of triggers as the buttons that get pushed, sending your emotions into overdrive. Maybe it's a certain classmate's comment that always rubs you the wrong way, or perhaps it's the pressure of upcoming exams that sends your stress levels soaring.

Whatever it is, take note of those triggers and the patterns that follow. Once you start connecting the dots between what sets you off and how you react, you'll be better equipped to navigate those emotional minefields with ease. So, next time you feel yourself getting fired up or down in the dumps, pause for a moment and ask yourself: What triggered this feeling? Is this a familiar pattern?

By shining a light on those triggers and patterns, you'll be well on your way to mastering the art of emotional self-awareness.

## 62. Healthy Coping Strategies

Developing healthy coping strategies – because life's twists and turns are a whole lot easier to navigate when you've got a toolbox full of healthy coping skills at your disposal.

When the going gets tough – whether it's a bad grade, a fight with a friend, or just a bad day – having go-to coping strategies can make all the difference. So, what are healthy coping strategies, you ask?

Well, they're the activities and techniques that help you deal with stress, manage your emotions, and bounce back from setbacks in a positive way. From going for a run to journaling your thoughts, talking to a trusted friend, or practicing mindfulness, there are tons of healthy coping strategies out there – it's all about finding what works best for you.

Coping Toolbox

- Deep Breathing: Practice simple breathing exercises to calm your mind and reduce stress.
- Journaling: Write down your thoughts and feelings to help process emotions and gain clarity.

- Mindfulness Meditation: Take a few minutes each day to practice mindfulness and focus on the present moment.
- Physical Activity: Engage in activities like going for a walk, dancing, or practicing yoga to release pent-up tension and boost mood.
- Creative Expression: Express yourself through art, music, or writing to channel emotions in a positive way.
- Talking to a Friend: Reach out to a trusted friend or family member for support and perspective.
- Time in Nature: Spend time outdoors to recharge and gain perspective away from screens and stressors.
- Positive Affirmations: Repeat positive affirmations to boost self-esteem and shift negative thinking patterns.

## 63. Build a Support System

Let's talk about how important it is to get help and build a strong support system. You don't have to deal with your feelings on your own.

Your support system is like your own personal cheerleading group. They'll be there to cheer you on when you're down and share in your joy when you succeed.

Having people who care about your well-being on your side, like friends, family, teachers, or even adults you trust, can make all the difference. That being said, don't be shy about asking for help when you're having a hard time. Know that there are people who will listen, offer a couch to cry on, or just hang out with you.

Don't be afraid to look into tools like counsellors, hotlines, or support groups if you ever feel like you need extra help. It's a sign of strength to ask for help when you need it. One comforting hug at a time, we'll get through the ups and downs of life's emotional roller coaster.

64. Take a Breath

Taking a moment to slow down and breathe can work wonders for your mental and emotional well-being.

Mindfulness is all about being present in the moment, tuning into your thoughts and feelings without judgment. It's like hitting the pause button on life's hectic soundtrack and giving yourself permission to just be. So, whether it's taking a few deep breaths, practicing simple meditation exercises, or doing a body scan to check in with how you're feeling, there are tons of ways to bring mindfulness into your daily routine.

And as for relaxation techniques, think of them as your secret weapons for melting away stress and tension. From progressive muscle relaxation to visualization exercises, there's a whole toolbox of relaxation techniques just waiting for you to explore. So, next time you're feeling frazzled or overwhelmed, why not give mindfulness and relaxation a try? Trust me, your mind and body will thank you for it.

## 65. Boundaries for your Emotions

Knowing your limits and communicating them to others is a superpower that can help you navigate life's ups and downs with grace and confidence. Setting boundaries means drawing a line in the sand and saying, "This is what I'm comfortable with, and this is what I'm not."

It's about honoring your own needs and values, even if it means saying no to others or stepping back from certain situations.

Whether it's telling a friend you need space, setting screen time limits to protect your mental health, or standing up for yourself when someone crosses a line, boundaries are all about taking care of yourself and showing others how you deserve to be treated.

So, don't be afraid to speak up and set boundaries that support your emotional well-being – you deserve to feel safe, respected, and valued in all your relationships and interactions.

66. Seeking Professional Help

Whether you're struggling with overwhelming emotions, facing mental health issues, or dealing with difficult situations, reaching out to a trained professional can be a game-changer.

Therapists, counselors, and mental health professionals are there to provide support, guidance, and a safe space to explore your thoughts and feelings without judgment. It's like having a trusted ally in your corner, helping you navigate life's twists and turns with strength and resilience.

So, if you ever find yourself struggling to cope or feeling like you're at a loss, remember that it's okay to ask for help. Seeking professional support isn't a sign of weakness – it's a brave and empowering step towards prioritizing your well-being and creating a brighter future for yourself.

You deserve to feel happy, healthy, and supported, so don't hesitate to reach out and take that first step towards healing.

## 67. Social Influences

Navigating social influences can sometimes feel like navigating a maze – full of twists, turns, and unexpected challenges.

As teenagers, we're bombarded with messages from peers, social media, and society about how we should look, act, and think. It's easy to get swept up in the pressure to fit in or conform to unrealistic standards, but it's important to remember that you have the power to chart your own course.

Take a step back, tune into your values and beliefs, and ask yourself what truly matters to you. Surround yourself with people who lift you up, support your dreams, and celebrate your uniqueness.

Remember, you don't have to follow the crowd or please everyone – the most important thing is staying true to yourself and embracing who you are. So, stand tall, march to the beat of your own drum, and let your individuality shine bright.

## 68. Being Emotionally Strong

You can't be emotionally strong by always acting like everything is fine. You have to be honest about how you feel, face problems head-on, and find good ways to deal with them and grow from them.

Like working out a muscle, the more you do it, the stronger it gets. So, don't be afraid to face your fears, accept your weaknesses, and ask for help when you need it.

Spend time with encouraging people, take care of yourself, and remember that setbacks are just temporary problems that will get you to your goals.

## 69. Connecting with Nature

There's something inherently soothing about being in nature – the rustle of leaves, the warmth of the sun, the gentle rhythm of waves crashing against the shore.

Spending time outdoors can provide a much-needed escape from the hustle of daily life, giving you space to breathe, reflect, and reconnect with yourself.

Whether it's going for a hike, taking a leisurely stroll through the park, spending time outdoors can be a powerful way to find inner peace.

## 70. Expressing Yourself Creatively

Sometimes, words alone aren't enough to capture the complexity of our emotions. Whether it's through art, music, writing, or other forms of creative expression, finding a healthy outlet for your feelings can be incredibly cathartic.

So, grab a paintbrush, strum a guitar, or let your pen dance across the page – there's no right or wrong way to express yourself creatively, as long as it helps you process and release what's on your mind!

# CHAPTER EIGHT

## PARENTS & SIBLINGS

71. Relationship with Your Parents

How to get to a whole new level of relationship and understanding.

You can build a strong relationship with your parents by talking to them in an open and honest way, where both of you feel heard and respected.

Active listening is one of the most important skills you can learn. That means paying attention to what your parents are saying without stopping or making assumptions.

Remember that conversation goes both ways, so be ready to hear their point of view and find things you can agree on. Fostering open communication and mutual respect will not only make your relationship with your parents stronger, but it will also help you learn important life skills that will help you in the long run.

## 72. Conflict with Siblings

Let's face it – conflicts with siblings are practically a rite of passage. But here's the thing: learning how to navigate these disagreements can actually strengthen your relationship and teach you valuable life skills.

When tensions rise, it's important to keep a cool head and approach the situation with an open mind. One effective strategy is compromise – finding a middle ground that satisfies both parties.

Negotiation is another key tool in your conflict resolution toolbox – listening to each other's perspectives, expressing your own needs, and working together to find a solution that feels fair to everyone involved.

And don't forget about setting boundaries – establishing clear rules and expectations can help prevent conflicts from escalating in the first place. By practicing compromise, negotiation, and boundary-setting, you'll not only resolve conflicts with your siblings more effectively but also build stronger, more harmonious relationships that last a lifetime

## 73. Positive Relationships with Family

It all starts with trust, the foundation of any solid relationship. Show your parents and siblings that you're reliable, honest, and there for them when they need you.

And speaking of being there, empathy is key – try to see things from their perspective and lend a supportive ear when they're going through a rough patch.

Mutual respect is another biggie – treat your family members the way you'd like to be treated, even when you don't see eye to eye.

Remember, relationships take work, but the payoff is totally worth it – a tribe of people who've got your back no matter what. So, sprinkle some trust, empathy, and respect into your family dynamic, and watch those bonds grow stronger every day.

## 74. Sharing Responsibilities

Let's talk about being responsible for each other at home. It's not just about work, trust me. It's not only a way to keep the house clean to help out around the house.

It's also a chance to show your family that you're ready to take on the world with them. First, make a list of what needs to be done and give everyone a fair share of the work.

For example, your sibling might be in charge of vacuuming, and your parents might be in charge of food shopping. No matter how you divide up the work in your home, understand that everyone's contribution is important.

Sharing responsibilities not only keeps things going smoothly, but it also helps you become more independent and work better with others, which are skills that will help you in every part of your life. Put on your work gloves, help out, and watch your family grow as you do each job together.

75. Respecting Differences

Let's dive into the awesome world of respecting differences within your family – because variety truly is the spice of life! Think about it: your family is made up of a bunch of unique individuals, each with their own quirks, interests, and perspectives. And that's what makes them so special!

Embracing these differences isn't just about tolerating them – it's about celebrating them and recognizing that they're what make your family so awesome. Whether it's your sister's love for punk rock, your dad's obsession with gardening, or your mom's knack for dad jokes, take the time to appreciate what makes each family member unique.

By fostering a sense of acceptance and inclusivity, you'll create a home where everyone feels valued and respected for who they are. So, rock on with your differences, embrace the quirks, and watch your family bond grow stronger than ever before. You're all in this together!

76. Dynamics

Family dynamics – it's like unraveling a mystery where everyone has a unique role to play! Ever wonder why your older sibling is always so bossy, or why your parents have different expectations for you and your younger brother?

Understanding these dynamics is key to navigating family life like a pro. Birth order, for example, can shape your personality and how you interact with your siblings. And let's not forget about parental expectations – they're like the unwritten rules that govern your family's behavior and values.

Oh, and cultural influences? They're like the secret sauce that adds flavor to your family dynamic, whether it's celebrating holidays or passing down traditions from generation to generation. By unraveling these complexities and understanding how they shape your family, you'll gain valuable insights into how to navigate family life with confidence and grace.

## 77. Quality Time

The importance of quality time with your fam squad – it's like hitting pause on the chaos of life and soaking in those precious moments together!

Whether it's game nights with your siblings, movie marathons with your parents, or just chilling and chatting over dinner, carving out dedicated time to hang with the fam is key to building strong bonds and creating memories that'll last a lifetime.

It's about more than just being in the same room – it's about truly connecting, laughing, and making each other feel loved and valued.

So, next time you're tempted to scroll through social media or binge-watch Netflix solo, why not invite your family to join in the fun? Trust me, those moments spent together are what life's all about.

78. Having each others back

Let's talk about having each other's backs – it's like being part of an epic team where everyone's got a role to play!

Whether it's cheering on your sibling at their soccer game or being there for your friend during a tough breakup, supporting each other is what makes us stronger together.

It's about lending a listening ear when someone needs to vent, offering a shoulder to cry on when things get tough, and giving each other that extra boost of confidence when we're feeling down.

Remember, we're all in this crazy journey called life together, and having someone to lean on can make all the difference. So, don't hesitate to reach out to your squad when you need a little extra love and support – because that's what friends and family are for!

79. Resolutions

Let's chat about resolving those occasional family squabbles – it's like finding the right emoji to diffuse a tense situation!

Whether it's about who left the dishes in the sink or whose turn it is to walk the dog, family issues can sometimes feel like a never-ending game of tug-of-war.

But guess what? With a little patience, communication, and willingness to compromise, you can totally tackle these challenges like a boss. Instead of letting things simmer under the surface, speak up, and address the problem head-on.

Remember, it's not about winning or being right – it's about finding common ground and working together to maintain harmony within the household. So, next time you're faced with a family issue, take a deep breath, put on your problem-solving hat, and get ready to find a solution that works for everyone.

# CHAPTER NINE

## PERSONAL HEALTH & GROOMING

### 80. Daily Hygiene

First up, we've got bathing – whether you're a quick shower ninja or a long soak lover, make sure to scrub-a-dub-dub with soap and water to wash away the day's grime.

Next, dental care – no one likes a funky breath monster, so grab that toothbrush and paste and give those pearly whites a good scrub twice a day.

And let's not forget skincare – whether you're battling breakouts or aiming for that glowing complexion, a simple routine of cleansing and moisturizing can work wonders.

So, whether you're hitting the books, hanging with friends, or crushing it on the sports field, remember to make time for these daily hygiene practices – because feeling fresh and clean is always a win!

## 81. Exercise & Physical Activity

Let's move and groove—it's like putting on your favourite song and dancing like no one's looking!

Being active and working out isn't just about getting six-pack abs or bench pressing your own body weight; it's also about feeling great all around.

Whether you like dancing, shooting hoops with friends, or going for a jog in the park, finding things you enjoy to do can make it easy to stay active.

Aside from keeping your body in great shape, daily exercise is also great for your mood. It gives you a natural high and helps get rid of those pesky stress monsters. Put on your trainers and your favourite workout clothes, and let's make staying fit and beautiful a daily habit. After all, you can handle anything that comes your way!

## 82. Drugs & Alcohol

Yes, kids, let's talk about something serious: drug use and abuse. It's like being in charge of your own ship and staying out of trouble!

We understand that the need to fit in or feel cool can make trying drugs, alcohol, or tobacco seem appealing. But you need to know what the risks are before you take that jump.

Substance abuse can hurt your health, make it harder to make decisions, and mess up your relationships and plans for the future.

So, think about how that smoke or drink might affect your life before you light up or sip. Always remember that you have the power to make choices, and being smart about how you use drugs is one of the best ways to protect your health and well-being.

You should never be afraid to talk to a trusted adult or a service if you're having trouble or need help. Your health and happiness are worth it!

83. Sleep Health

It's like giving your batteries a boost, so you can face each day with energy and excitement!

We know that staying up late to study, read through social media, or watch all of your favourite shows in one sitting can make you want to skip sleep.

However, getting enough good sleep is very important for your health and well-being as a whole. Getting into good sleep habits, which is also called "sleep hygiene," can really help.

There are many things you can do to make your bedroom a better place to sleep, such as making it cool, dark, and quiet, and going to bed at the same time every night.

So, the next time you want to stay up late, remember that putting sleep first isn't just about feeling better; it's about giving your mind and body the rest they need to do well. Turn off those screens, get comfortable in bed and get ready to fall asleep. A good night's sleep is the best ability of all!

## 84. Check Ups

Let's talk about check-ups and screenings – they're like tuning up your car to keep it running smoothly, but for your body! We know that going to the doctor might not be the most exciting thing on your to-do list, but trust us, it's super important for your health and well-being.

Regular check-ups and screenings can help catch any potential health issues early on, before they have a chance to become bigger problems down the road.

From routine physical exams and vaccinations to screenings for things like blood pressure, cholesterol, and STIs, these appointments are all about keeping you in tip-top shape.

So, the next time your parents nag you about scheduling that check-up, remember that they've got your best interests at heart. Taking care of your health now will set you up for a lifetime of wellness and happiness – and that's definitely something worth prioritizing!

## 85. Nutrition

Eating well and having a good diet is like fueling up your favorite video game character for an epic quest, but for your body!

We get it, with so many tempting snacks and fast food options out there, it can be tempting to indulge in less-than-healthy choices. But here's the deal – eating a balanced diet rich in fruits, veggies, whole grains, and lean proteins is essential for keeping your body and mind in top shape.

Plus, making healthy food choices now will set you up for a lifetime of good health and happiness. So, the next time you're tempted to reach for that bag of chips or order that extra-large soda, think about how it will make you feel in the long run.

And remember, healthy eating isn't about deprivation – it's about nourishing your body with the nutrients it needs to thrive. So, load up on those colorful fruits and veggies, and get ready to feel amazing from inside out!

## 86. Body Image

Let's talk about building positive body image and self-esteem – it's like giving yourself a high-five in the mirror every morning!

We know that growing up can sometimes feel like a rollercoaster ride, especially when it comes to how we see ourselves. But here's the scoop – you're amazing just the way you are, from head to toe. Embracing your unique quirks, flaws, and all the things that make you, well, you, is the key to rocking that confidence like a boss.

So, the next time you catch yourself comparing yourself to someone else or picking apart your appearance, take a moment to remind yourself of all the incredible things that make you shine.

Whether it's your killer sense of humor, your passion for your favorite hobby, or the way you always know how to make your friends laugh, you've got so much to celebrate. So, stand tall, own your awesomeness, and remember – you're one of a kind, and that's pretty darn special!

## 87. Personal Safety

Let's chat about personal safety and self-care – it's like giving yourself a big virtual hug every day!

We know life can get hectic sometimes, but taking care of yourself should always be a top priority. From looking both ways before crossing the street to trusting your gut instincts in unfamiliar situations, practicing personal safety is all about being smart and staying aware of your surroundings.

And when it comes to self-care, think of it as filling up your own cup so you can pour into others. Whether it's taking a break from social media to unwind, practicing mindfulness to calm your mind, or simply taking a few deep breaths when things feel overwhelming, finding what works for you is key.

So, take a moment to check in with yourself each day, and remember – you're worth taking care of, inside and out!

## 88. Stress Management

Stress management – because keeping cool under pressure is like being your own superhero! We get it, life can throw some curveballs, from school deadlines to social drama, and everything in between.

But here's the deal – stress is a natural part of life, and learning how to handle it like a pro can make all the difference. So, whether it's taking a breather with some deep belly breaths, going for a walk to clear your mind, or jamming out to your favorite tunes, finding what helps you chill out is key.

And hey, don't forget to reach out to a trusted friend, family member, or even a professional if things start feeling too overwhelming. You're not alone, and there's always someone ready to lend an ear or offer some support. So, take a deep breath, remember that you've got this, and keep on shining bright!

# CHAPTER TEN

## DEVELOP A GROWTH MINDSET

89. Growth Mindset

Ever wondered why some people seem to bounce back from challenges easily while others get stuck?

It's all about mindset!

Picture this: a fixed mindset says, "I'm either good at something or I'm not," while a growth mindset believes, "I can improve with effort and practice."

Think of it like this: imagine you're playing a video game. With a fixed mindset, you might give up if you can't beat a level on the first try.

But with a growth mindset, you'd keep trying, learning from each attempt until you conquer that level. See, it's not about being perfect; it's about the journey of improvement.

So, let's unlock that growth mindset and tackle challenges head-on!

## 90. SMART Goals

Ever feel like you're spinning your wheels, not sure where you're headed?

That's where SMART goals come in! Imagine this: you've got a dream, like acing your exams, starting a YouTube channel, or running a 5K.

Instead of just saying, "I wanna do better in school," or "I'll start a channel someday," you break it down.

SMART goals are Specific (like "I'll study for one hour every day"), Measurable (you can track your progress with grades or subscribers), Achievable (realistic steps you can take), Relevant (aligning with what you want), and Time-bound (with deadlines, like acing that test by next month).

So, let's ditch the vague dreams and turn them into action-packed SMART goals that'll take you places!

## 91. Positive Attitude

Ever feel like the universe is throwing lemons your way, and you're just not feeling the lemonade vibe? It's all about that positive attitude!

Picture this: you bomb a test, or your crush doesn't text back. Instead of spiraling into negativity, think of it like this: setbacks are just detours on the road to success.

Sure, you might stumble, but with a positive attitude, you'll bounce back stronger. It's like having a secret superpower that turns obstacles into opportunities.

So, let's flip the script and see those challenges as chances to grow and shine brighter than ever.

Some affirmations to get you going! But try to write some of your own.

"I am capable of achieving my goals, no matter how big they may seem."

"I believe in myself and my abilities to overcome any challenge that comes my way."

## 92. Mistakes

Learning from mistakes is like discovering hidden treasure in the rough patches of life. It's all about that growth mindset, where setbacks become stepping stones toward success.

Picture this: you try out for the school play and totally flub your audition. Instead of wallowing in embarrassment, you take a deep breath, dust yourself off, and think, "What can I learn from this?"

Maybe you realize you need to practice more or work on your stage presence. Each stumble becomes a chance to sharpen your skills and grow stronger.

So, embrace those slip-ups, because each one is a golden opportunity to level up and shine even brighter!

93. Curiosity

Ever wonder what's beyond the horizon or what makes the universe tick?

Nurturing your curiosity is like opening the door to a world of endless possibilities. It's about asking those "what ifs" and diving headfirst into the unknown with an insatiable hunger for knowledge.

Whether it's delving into the mysteries of science, unraveling the threads of history, or uncovering the secrets of the cosmos, curiosity fuels your journey of discovery.

So, don't be afraid to let your imagination run wild and follow your wonder wherever it may lead. Who knows? You just might stumble upon the next big idea that changes the world!

## 94. Overcoming Self Doubt

Ever felt like you're standing on the edge of something big, but that little voice inside your head says, "You can't do it"?

Welcome to the club!

Overcoming self-doubt is like flexing your mental muscles – it takes practice, patience, and a whole lot pep talks. It's about squashing those pesky doubts and replacing them with a big ol' dose of "I've got this!"

Sure, it's easier said than done, but with each small victory, you'll feel that confidence grow stronger. So, next time self-doubt comes knocking, show it who's boss!

You're capable, you're resilient, and you're destined for greatness. Believe it, because you've got what it takes to conquer anything that comes your way!

## 95. Celebrating Wins

Let's talk about celebrating your wins, big or small.

Every step forward, every hurdle overcome, deserves a little celebration. It's about acknowledging the effort you've put in and the progress you've made.

Maybe you aced that tough math test you were stressing over, or perhaps you finally nailed that guitar riff you've been practicing for weeks.

Whatever it is, take a moment to pat yourself on the back and do a little happy dance! Celebrating your growth isn't just about the end result – it's about recognizing the hard work and dedication you've poured into becoming the amazing person you are today.

So, go ahead, treat yourself to some ice cream, blast your favorite song, and bask in the glow of your awesomeness. You've earned it!

## 96. Embrace Change

In a world that's constantly evolving, being adaptable is a crucial survival skill. It's about being open to new experiences, facing challenges head-on, and finding creative solutions to unexpected situations

As a teen, you're already navigating a period of significant change in your life, from transitioning to new schools to exploring career paths.

Embracing change means being willing to step out of your comfort zone, try new things, and learn from every experience, whether it's a success or a setback. It's about recognizing that change is inevitable and seeing it as an opportunity for growth and personal development.

So, embrace change with an open mind and a positive attitude, knowing that it's all part of your journey towards becoming the best version of yourself.

## 97. Persistence

As a teenager, you're bound to encounter challenges along the way — whether it's struggling with a tough assignment, facing rejection, or feeling discouraged.

But it's important to remember that setbacks are not failures; they're opportunities to learn and grow. By cultivating persistence and perseverance, you develop the resilience to keep pushing forward, even when things get tough.

So, don't be afraid to put in the effort, keep trying, and never give up on your dreams. With the right mindset and a willingness to keep going, you'll be amazed at what you can achieve.

## 98. Feedback

A growth mindset involves embracing feedback as a valuable tool for learning and growth.

Instead of fearing criticism or viewing it as a sign of failure, see it as an opportunity to improve and become better at what you do.

As a teenager navigating the complexities of life, you'll encounter plenty of situations where feedback plays a crucial role – whether it's from teachers, coaches, peers, or even yourself.

By actively seeking feedback and being open to constructive criticism, you show a willingness to learn and evolve. Remember, nobody starts off as an expert, and everyone has room for improvement. So, don't shy away from feedback; embrace it, learn from it, and use it to propel yourself forward on your journey of personal growth and development.

99. Embrace the Journey

Life is an adventure filled with twists, turns, ups, and downs. Embrace every experience, whether it's a success or a setback, as an opportunity to learn, grow, and become the best version of yourself.

Stay curious, stay resilient, and never lose sight of your dreams and aspirations.

Remember, the journey is just as important as the destination, so cherish every moment, stay true to yourself, and keep moving forward with confidence and determination.

With the right mindset and a willingness to adapt and overcome, you'll be well-equipped to conquer any challenge that comes your way.

100. Points to Remember

1. Set Realistic Goals: Break down large tasks into smaller, manageable goals. Celebrate each milestone to build confidence and momentum.
2. Embrace Mistakes: View mistakes as opportunities to learn. Reflect on what went wrong and how to improve next time.
3. Seek Feedback: Actively seek out feedback and use it constructively. Understand that feedback is a tool for growth, not a judgment of ability.
4. Stay Curious: Pursue new interests and hobbies. Cultivate a passion for learning and discovery.
5. Practice Self-Compassion: Be kind to yourself. Understand that growth takes time, and setbacks are a natural part of the process.

## 101. You Got This!

Remember, you're stronger and more resilient than you think.

Life will throw challenges your way, but with the right mindset, skills, and support network, you have the power to overcome them and emerge even stronger.

Trust in yourself, stay adaptable, and never underestimate the value of perseverance.

Your potential is limitless – go out there and seize it!

Printed in Great Britain
by Amazon

43697836R00066